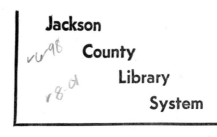

all color book of

Flowers

*100 color photographs of spectacular
flowers of the world*

Moira Savonius

octopus
Octopus Books

First published 1974 by
Octopus Books Limited
59 Grosvenor Street, London W1

ISBN 0 7064 0324 X

© 1974 Octopus Books Limited

Produced by Mandarin Publishers Limited
14 Westlands Road, Quarry Bay, Hong Kong

Printed in Hong Kong

Contents

Introduction

The richness and variety of the world's plant life is so immense that no single publication could ever do it justice. The flowers mentioned and illustrated in this book only show a few examples of some of the different plant families that make up the vegetation of the five continents. Nearly a quarter of a million flowering plants are known and recorded and more are still being discovered. Some are extremely rare and local, while others range over huge areas, but apart from the frozen wastes of the Antarctic, high mountain tops and certain desert areas, flowers of one kind or another are found all over the world and every species is adapted to its natural environment.

All flowers, ranging from the common daisy to flamboyant tropical climbers, have a beauty of their own, and often the appeal of a small and simple wild flower is greater than that of a highly sophisticated man-made hybrid. The love of flowers goes back thousands of years in the history of mankind, and wherever there have been settled civilizations in the world, flowers have been used for religious or purely aesthetic purposes. In ancient Egypt and in China, in Persia and in the Aztec and Inca kingdoms of the Americas flowers were held in high esteem and it was in these places, rather than in Europe, that the cultivation of flowers first began.

There are still plenty of wild flowers in the world, but they have decreased alarmingly during the last two centuries, and will undoubtedly continue to do so with the increase of urban development and intensive cultivation of food crops. Many species are known to be threatened with extinction and often they are so difficult to grow anywhere except in their native habitat that they cannot even be saved through the efforts of horticulturists. The concentrated grazing of domestic live stock, extensive fires, the draining of marshes and the felling of forests, as well as the excessive use of herbicides and the commercial exploitation of rare plants such as tropical orchids, have contributed to the loss.

The wild flowers of the world are a precious heritage. Once lost they are irreplaceable. Man with all his cleverness cannot create a new species. He can breed and select and hybridize and change the appearance of plants profoundly, and sometimes it seems that he goes too far and the results become garish and vulgar. It might perhaps be better if we paid more attention to the preservation of original wild species and resisted the temptation to improve them. Generations to come might well be more thankful for a wide and varied flora of wild plants than for too many opulent gladioli and enormous marigolds.

All the flowers illustrated in this book are given their full scientific names and the name of the botanical family to which they belong. Popular names alone would only cause confusion, but the use of two Latin names, the first indicating the genus and the second establishing the exact species, identify a plant beyond doubt and are accepted the world over.

Right Honeydew lily; see page 70.

Bluebell *Endymion non-scriptus* Family Liliaceae

This flower grows in many parts of Western Europe, especially in France, but it is in England that it reaches its greatest glory and it is often called the English bluebell. Bluebell woods in May are one of the sights of the countryside and the soft, rich colouring of the massed flowers beneath the tender green of newly unfolded leaves has a wonderfully soothing effect on frayed nerves. The flowers spring each year from perennial bulbs and they also seed themselves abundantly and are easily naturalized, but they quickly wilt and lose their beauty if picked.

Flowers that change the landscape

It is not in the rampant vegetation of tropical jungles that the most colourful displays of flowers are to be seen. A hot, moist climate encourages the development of foliage, but the flowers seldom dominate the picture, although individually they may be both beautiful and bright. The flowers that really change a landscape occur either in northern climates or in rather arid, perhaps even semi-desert areas. Here for a short time after the spring rains they appear in profusion, blossoming and seeding, and then vanishing again until the following year.

Sometimes this profuse flowering may not even be a regular annual occurrence. In countries subject to severe droughts for example, a long time may pass before another good season. Many seeds are capable of lying dormant for years in the soil and then they all germinate together when conditions are right. Bulbous plants can also bide their time like this, and there are others which mature very slowly. In this way years may pass between one spectacular flowering and the next.

Changes in the environment can often bring about an unexpected flowering from dormant seeds. These changes can be caused by extensive fires or a disturbance of the soil surface, usually brought about by man's interference. The seeds may have been lying buried in the soil too deep for germination, or may have been wind-borne to the site and found the new conditions congenial to growth. The tremendous blaze of scarlet poppies in Flanders during the first world war was caused by the shelling and trench digging which exposed previously buried layers of soil. The beautiful rich pink willowherb or fireweed spreads rapidly on bomb sites, or after forest fires, because of its ability to colonize open spaces by wind-blown seeds which germinate and grow particularly well in ashes.

There have also been many instances of introduced plants literally taking over a new environment and in a very short time changing the appearance of a landscape where they were previously unknown. Australian acacias in southern Europe and South Africa, the Asiatic *Rhododendron ponticum* in the British Isles, the viper's bugloss introduced to Australia, have all become established far from their native habitat. In many instances the introduction of foreign plants, either deliberately or unwittingly, has been unfortunate. This is because they have grown so much more rampantly in their new surroundings than in their native countries that they have become unmanageable weeds. The poisonous ragwort, which was introduced to Australia and New Zealand, quickly ruined grazing grounds. The South American *lantana camara*, a shrubby plant with attractive flowers, became a thorough nuisance in Hawaii until its progress was restrained by the introduction of certain insects which were able to keep it in check.

As far as wild flowers are concerned, man's intervention has usually done more harm than good. The more progressive farming methods are, the more uniform and uninteresting the landscape becomes. Cereals and root crops, sugar cane and banana plantations, tea and coffee gardens, rice paddies, tobacco fields and most of the other commercial crops are far from colourful. Here and there the blazing yellow of mustard and rape, the fields of commercially grown flowers or the blossoming of orchards and almond trees in spring will give a bonus of colour even to an intensely cultivated landscape. A fine show of wild flowers, however, is something to be sought on poor land unfit for cultivation, for instance on abandoned waste ground or in remote areas where climate and soil make agricultural effort uneconomic. The heather moors of the north, the arid creosote bush country of Mexico, the flowering high alpine slopes where snow falls early and lies late, and the hot dry veldt of South Africa and plains of Australia: these are all places where plants which are truly adapted to their environment will thrive and blossom in full splendour in their season.

Many of the wild flowers which can make a tremendous impact in the mass are quite small and insignificant in themselves, and in a garden setting they might well be scorned as weeds. Quite a few are in fact weeds, and because they spread rapidly by seeds and runners they are not generally welcomed in gardens. The common buttercup and the little lawn daisy, the dandelion and the speedwell, are all under constant attack when they intrude where they are not wanted. Yet when they are seen in large numbers in a country field or on waste land they undoubtedly add beauty to the landscape.

Because of the way in which they catch and reflect light, white flowers show up particularly well against a green background, on bare ground, and among fallen leaves. The wood anemones of the northern forests, the white scented poet's narcissus of the Grecian plains, the masses of Queen Anne's Lace which floats like froth on the green sea of the country fields, are three quite different white wild flowers. Each one of them in its season transforms the place where it grows.

Bluebells, purple heather, golden gorse, sunny Californian poppies, and many more of the world's wild flowers can change and dominate a landscape, giving it a colour and character which is lost again when their flowering comes to an end. It is this pageant of the seasons, in its brief and impressive glory, that makes the world an exciting place to explore.

Left
Lupin *Lupinus ornatus* Family
Leguminosae
Very few of the world's deserts are
completely barren, and although they
may be quite unsuitable for cultivation,
they often sustain a number of plants
which have become adapted to the
conditions. The Arizona desert, for
example, is famous for its unique
character and its innumerable spiny cacti,
including the deceptively furry looking
chollas in this picture. In a rainy season,
such as the spring of 1973, many other
plants come into flower and here lupins
have softened the harsh desert landscape
with a haze of blue.

Below left
Gorse *Ulex europaeus* Family
Leguminosae
This prickly shrub grows throughout
western Europe and Britain, often along
cliff tops and in poor sandy soils. It is
seldom out of flower and when in full
bloom it makes a tremendous impact on
the landscape. Linnaeus, the father of
botany, knelt in tears when he first saw
its golden splendour and it looks even
more beautiful by the blue sea or among
purple heather. The flowers have a strong
almond scent and later the seeds explode
from the ripe pods with an audible
crackle. The impenetrable thickets
provide shelter for many nesting birds,
which also feed on the seeds.

Top right
Dandelion *Taraxacum officinale* Family
Compositae
This is one of the commonest plants of
the northern temperate zone both in the
old and the new world. If it were rare it
would be eagerly sought and treasured for
the bright flower that rises on a hollow
stalk from branching perennial roots.
The delicate globes of downy seeds that
succeed the flowers, quickly sending their
parachutes flying away on the wind, are
fascinating and just as lovely in their own
way. The dandelions of Siberia are said
to be especially large and fine and as in
other countries, the leaves are eaten as
salad and the roots are roasted and used
for making substitute coffee.

Right
Thrift *Armeria maritima* Family
Plumbaginaceae
Many plants only grow wild in very
specialized localities, and the common
thrift or sea pink, although it will
transplant to gardens, is in nature always
found by the sea and often so close to the
water that it becomes covered in spray.
The thrifts which are sometimes seen in
mountains or even on inland heaths are
sub-species with differing characteristics.
The sea thrift is a European plant, found
both on rocky and sandy shores as well as
in salt marshes and when the vividly pink
flowers are in their prime during early
summer they completely change the
appearance of the scene.

11

Left

Wild Daffodil *Narcissus pseudo-narcissus*
Family Amaryllidaceae
The wild daffodil or lent lily is found in
many parts of Europe, including England,
where it appears to be a native plant and
still occurs in large numbers in certain
localities. It is one of the earliest of the
spring flowers, giving the landscape life
and colour before the grass has begun to
grow or the trees have come into leaf.
The Pyrenean mountain valleys are also
famous for their wonderful displays of
daffodils and it is from here that the
parents of the many fine garden
varieties have come.

Below left

Sheep's sorrel *Rumex acetocella* Family
Polygonaceae
This picture, taken in southern Portugal,
shows how a plant, so insignificant that a
single specimen would hardly be noticed
by anyone but a botanist, can yet
completely dominate the landscape when
it proliferates as it has done here.
Sheep's sorrel seldom grows more than
six inches high and the individual
flowers are minute, but on poor acid
soils it often spreads very fast and when
previously cultivated land is lying fallow,
as was the case in this locality, the whole
area becomes covered in a mantle of red.

Right

Butterfly flower *Schizanthus pinnatus*
Family Solanaceae
The South American butterfly flowers,
which are also often called poor man's
orchid because of the intricate and
beautiful patterning of the petals, are
quite well known in their hybrid form
as greenhouse annuals. Here they are
pictured growing wild in Chile, covering
the ground in a dense, rosy lilac carpet.
In the wild they are more compact than
under cultivation and the rather fragile
stems support each other and keep the
flowers upright. In early summer large
patches of their rich colouring give a
special beauty to many Chilean valleys.

Right

Viper's bugloss *Echium plantagineum*
Family Boraginaceae
This is a Mediterranean plant, but the
photograph was taken in Australia where
it was introduced as a garden flower on a
farm belonging to a family named
Paterson, in New South Wales. It was
first noticed on the nearby stock route
in 1896 and from there it spread with
amazing rapidity, and in eight years
travelled more than 500 miles from its
original point of introduction. It
changed the landscape profoundly, and
many an Australian valley now looks like
a vivid blue lake during the flowering
season. Unfortunately it is also a serious
weed in the pastures and is known as
Paterson's curse, blue weed, blue devil,
and rather surprisingly also as salvation
Jane.

Above and left
Californian poppy *Eschscholzia
californica* Family Papaveraceae
Like so many other wild flowers this
brilliant annual is nothing like as common
now as it was when it was first seen
carpeting the hills of California by the
Spaniards. Here and there however,
especially in the regions near San
Francisco, it can still provide a wonderful
display when the four-petalled flowers
throw off their pointed green caps and
open to the sun. There are several closely
related species, some of them perennial
and all native to the Pacific coast of
North America. The common annual with
grey-green finely divided leaves which
grows well as a garden plant is variable,
and many different forms have been
raised, including some with double
flowers.

Right
Platdoring flowers *Grielum sp* Family
Rosaceae
The arid veldt of the north western Cape
Province in South Africa often appears to
be virtually desert land, with only a few
evergreen shrubs to give a semblance of
life, but in certain seasons after good
spring rains, the whole area is transformed and becomes so beautiful that
tourists flock there to admire the floral
display. Among the many different
flowers which suddenly appear are the
Grielum species, members of the rose
family, with finely dissected leaves. In
many places they form a carpet which
stretches for miles over the red earth.

Europe

Right
Ramonda nathalie Family Gesneriaceae
The charming ramondas are shade-loving
plants which normally grow in rock
crevices, in ravines and on slopes facing
north. They are intolerant of direct
sunlight and need moisture combined
with sharp drainage. Their European
distribution is curiously interrupted. The
species illustrated here is found in
Northern Greece and in Serbia. *Ramonda
serbica*, whose flowers have blue anthers
instead of yellow ones, is a native of
Serbia and Albania and the third species,
Ramonda myconi which is a larger plant
with pale mauve flowers, only grows in
the Pyrenees and has long been in
cultivation as a garden plant.

Compared to the continents with a warmer climate, Europe is poor in plant species. However many of the flowers of this region have great charm and delicacy and their comparatively small stature sets them apart from flamboyant tropical blooms. There are no real desert areas, and although the winter can be very cold in northern and central Europe, there are seldom long periods of drought and the spring and summer climate encourages the growth of plants from north of the Arctic Circle right down to the Mediterranean.

The flora of mountain areas in central Europe has a great affinity with the far north and many of the arctic flowers grow also in the Alps. The greater amount of summer light in the north compensates for the short growing season and the plants in Lapland consequently complete their annual growth cycle much more quickly than those growing further south. Although the arctic and alpine regions are by no means barren of vegetation, the range of plants is limited to those which can survive very low temperatures. Mosses, lichens, birch and willow scrub, heather, moss campions, mountain avens and arctic cinquefoil, cloudberries, cranberries and cotton grass are some of the plants that survive under these harsh conditions, protected to some extent by the snow which covers them before the really severe cold sets in.

The European climate is much milder along the Atlantic seaboard, especially in Britain and Ireland, than it is for example in Germany, Poland and Russia. The influence of the Ocean, which does not become icebound like the Baltic, and the warmth released by the Gulf Stream, gives a milder winter. In consequence one also gets a landscape that is more green all the year round than east of the Rhine, or along the Mediterranean coast where the hot summer dries up the grass and wild flowers by July. In the extreme south of Europe there is instead a season of late autumn flowers. This is almost a dress rehearsal for spring, which of course begins several months earlier than in the north.

The flowers that one finds in different parts of Europe depend very much on the soil. For example the flora of the chalk and limestone areas is richer and more varied than that of the poor sandy soils or the acid peats. The pine, spruce and birch woods of the north, the deciduous mixed woods of Britain and Central Europe, the beechwoods on the chalk, each have their own flora. The blue hepaticas, the almond-scented *Linnea*

borealis, the delicate pyrolas or wintergreens, and the low bilberry and cowberry shrubs and heather, are typical of the conifer woods of central Finland, Sweden and Norway. Further south their place is taken by white windflowers, spotted orchids and lilies of the valley. English woods are noted for their primroses and bluebells, violets and bramble blossom, while in Europe there are different kinds of anemones, hellebores, columbines and honeysuckles. In the dry pine and evergreen oak woods of southern Europe one finds an undergrowth of lavender and cistus shrubs, brooms, terrestrial orchids and wild cyclamen.

The flowers of the alpine slopes, such as the bright blue gentians and the pink primulas, the dwarf rhododendron, saxifragas and campanulas, are famous for their beauty, and in those places where natural meadows still exist there is a host of wild flowers which like to grow in the open in full sun. They belong to many different botanical families and have descendants or close relatives which have been grown as garden plants in Europe since the middle ages or earlier. Spring and autumn crocuses, lilies and ox-eye daisies, mallows, campions and meadow-sweet, knapweed and hawkweeds, along with many more well-loved flowers, are part of the European summer. In intensively cultivated areas most of these flowers have disappeared from the fields, but they are still found along boundary ditches and hedges, and along the margins of woods. Clovers and vetches abound on open downland, drainage ditches are often golden with marsh marigolds in the early spring, or thickly overhung with comfrey in summer, and many a cliff or limestone quarry is draped in pink when the valerian comes into bloom.

The charming briar roses and the big white convolvulus which scramble over hedges and fences, are a lovely sight, while the minor roads are fringed by the creamy or white flower heads of the various umbelliferous plants like hedge parsley, wild parsnip and the poisonous hemlock. Many an eyesore in waste places is hidden by such flowers as toadflax, mulleins, teazles, thistles and ragwort, as well as others which are often looked upon as weeds. Nevertheless they play their part in healing man-made scars very successfully, just like the willowherb.

The Mediterranean seaboard, where frost is a rare occurrence, has a different flora from the rest of Europe. Dwarf wild irises abound, there are scarlet anemones, wild stocks, scillas,

narcissus of many kinds, several pink and blue species of convolvulus, a number of spurges, stately fennel plants and beautiful asphodels. In Greece these tall flowers grow among the ruins
of ancient temples and towns, together with scarlet anemones
and poppies, little terrestrial orchids, several kinds of viper's
bugloss and the classical acanthus, whose decorative leaves were
used as the motif for the tops of Corinthian pillars.

In all the Mediterranean countries and islands, including
Portugal, the resinous smell of the pine trees and the fragrance
of blue lavender and rosemary blend with the aromatic scent of
the cistus bushes, whose masses of white, rose red or pink
flowers open in succession each morning and shed their petals
by the late afternoon. In Spain too the landscape is often
dominated by low spreading shrubs of yellow rock roses and

many different kinds of broom. Herbs like thyme, sage, basil
and savoury grow on the stony hillsides beside Mediterranean
heaths and fritillaries, bright blue lithospermum and anagallis,
and numerous terrestrial orchids.

All over Europe many naturalized plants have gained a foot-
hold and it is often difficult to tell for certain whether a flower
or a shrub is truly indigenous or not. Sometimes it is obviously
out of place, as in the case of the cacti and agaves along the
Mediterranean coast of Europe, but the almond tree has been
there so long that few people even think of it as originally
having arrived from the near east. The citrus family is now also
so well distributed all over the world that its ancient homeland,
south-east Asia, is all but forgotten.

Previous page
Blue Gentian *Gentiana clusii* Family
Gentianaceae
People tend to associate the gentians
especially with the Swiss Alps, but they
are also found on many other mountain
ranges both in Europe and in Asia. The
brilliance of their blue colouring varies,
but it is always beautiful. Many of them
are not easy to please in a garden and this
fact provides a challenge which alpine
enthusiasts are eager to accept. Gentians
need as much sunshine as possible, but
they also need constant moisture. This is
provided in their native habitat by the
melting snow which trickles through well-
drained stony soil to keep their roots
watered

Top left
Wild tulip *Tulipa bakeri* Family
Liliaceae
Most of the wild tulips are natives of
Turkey, Afghanistan and Persia, but
they also occur in Greece and on some
of the Mediterranean islands. There are
at least four endemic species on the
island of Crete, and all of them are
very beautiful plants. The one illustrated
here grows in rich ploughland amid the
White Mountains at the western end of
the island. It spreads by long fleshy roots
called stolons. The Cretans like to eat
boiled tulip bulbs, and they often find
their way into the local food markets at the
time of the spring ploughing.

Left
Red valerian *Centhranthus ruber* Family
Valerianaceae
One of the most impressive floral displays
of England is produced by this bold
plant, which clings precariously to the
white chalk cliffs by the sea. It also grows
in the shingle on the beach, in railway
cuttings or old chalk pits. In its native
Europe it is widespread and since
reaching England it has found localities
that suit it in places where few other
plants can gain a footing. It is grown as a
decorative plant in gardens, and in Italy
and Sicily the young leaves are served in
salads, in spite of their rather
unpleasantly pungent smell. The plant is
variable and there are forms with pink,
red or white flowers.

Right
Iris filifolia Family Iridaceae
This beautiful wild iris with the yellow
flecks on its crested falls is one of the
narrow-leaved irises which spring from a
bulbous root. Many of them grow in
Spain and this one was photographed on
the island of Málaga not far from the
Spanish coast. The bulbous irises form
two distinct groups, the short-stemmed
ones like *Iris histrioides* and *Iris
reticulata*, natives of Turkey and the
Caucasus, and the taller ones like this
which is a near relative of the cultivated
Spanish, English and Dutch irises. These
are derived from *Iris xiphiodes* and *Iris
xiphium,* both natives of Spain.

Left

Madonna lily *Lilium candidum* Family Liliaceae

This classic flower which in the Christian church became an emblem of purity associated with the Virgin Mary, is a native of the Balkans, but it has also been found growing wild in other parts of Europe. It is quite likely that it was distributed and planted by the Romans who used the bulb medicinally for healing wounds. The Madonna lily is noted for its strong scent and has always been a cherished garden plant. Like all the lilies it has an indefinable aristocratic air of quality which sets it apart from more common, gaudy flowers.

Below left

Mountain Primula *Primula hirsuta* Family Primulaceae

The primulas of the central European mountains are nearly all low in stature, and have unusually large flowers. This endearing characteristic has made them very popular among people who make collections of alpine plants, either out of doors or growing in pots in alpine houses. Like the plant in the photograph, many of these primulas can grow quite happily with the minimum of soil, as long as the crevice in which they have rooted can provide them with moisture. The long damp periods of the mild English winter does not suit them very well and they prefer to be covered in snow during their dormant season.

Top right

Pasque flower *Pulsatilla vulgaris* Family Ranunculaceae

The pasque flower, so called because in central Europe it usually flowers at Easter, is known in various forms throughout most of Europe. It grows in the far north, in Finland, and also in Italy, and it is thought that it may have been introduced to Britain by the Romans. The great charm of this plant lies in the silky hairiness of the stems and young leaves when the flowers first push up through the soil with bent heads. The colour of the flowers varies quite considerably in different forms, from pale lilac through rosy mauve to purple. They make good garden plants if left undisturbed.

Right

Blue pimpernel *Anagallis linifolia* Family Primulaceae

This little southern European plant rivals the blue of gentians and forms quite large hummocks which show up brilliantly against the often rather stony ground where it grows. Its narrow leaves are a dark, dull green and as the flowers begin to fade they turn crimson. It belongs to the same genus as the scarlet pimpernel, a weed from the arable land of Europe and also now of America. The clear scarlet flowers, which are sometimes blue instead, close quickly if the sun disappears behind clouds, and this has given the plant the name of poor man's weather glass.

Left
Ferula ferulago Family Umbelliferae
The ferulas are to a great extent natives of Southern Europe and belong to a group of plants which include several with medicinal uses. Their leaves are cut into fine, almost thread-like segments, and the tiny yellow flowers are gathered in clusters on numerous thin stalks which spring from one point at the top of the tall stems. In spite of these massive heads of bloom there is a light and graceful quality about the plants which makes them very distinctive, and well-grown plants in full bloom stand out boldly in the landscape.

Below left
Sunrose *Halimium allysoides* Family Cistaceae
The halimiums are a group of small, spreading shrubs with yellow flowers, found wild only in southern Europe round the Mediterranean, and in Spain and Portugal. As their common name implies, they are dependent on the sun like their larger relatives, the cistus species. The buds will only open in sunny weather and each individual flower lasts but a single day. The leaves are often grey and the shrubs are able to grow on very hot, dry hillsides, exposed to sea winds and strong sunlight. Several species have been brought into cultivation, but they need a warm sunny climate to thrive.

Right
Yellow asphodel *Asphodeline lutea* Family Liliaceae
This typical Mediterranean flower is also known as king's spear, or in southern France as *baton de jacob*. It differs from the white asphodels in having leaves all the way up the flowering stem, which grows about three feet tall. The numerous buds in the flower spike open in succession so that there is never as colourful a burst of bloom as one expects, but nevertheless it is a beautiful and interesting flower. The ancient Greeks used the roots for food and the plant was often mentioned in Greek literature but it does not take kindly to cultivation in colder climates. The yellow bog asphodel of Northern Europe is a different plant.

North America

Right
Columbine *Aquilegia flavescens* Family Ranunculaceae
Columbines are not confined to America but occur both in Europe and Asia as well, and have long been cultivated as garden flowers. They are very dainty and graceful, and the way the flowers hang nodding on the stalks adds to their charm. Several of the American columbines have longer spurs than those in the Old World, and the yellow and crimson colouring which is now found in the improved garden varieties is also derived from the American species. This beautiful yellow columbine is a native of Canada and the famous *Aquilegia caerulea*, with flowers of lavender and cream, is the floral emblem of the State of Colorado.

Botanically Canada has much in common with Scandinavia and Siberia in that a large area consists of rather flat coniferous forest land broken by numerous lakes. Despite the fact that the spruce trees and pines of Canada and the United States look very similar to those in Europe and Asia, they are not the same species. The same applies to many of the small shrubs and herbaceous plants, which are closely allied to species in the Old World, although the differences between them are enough to classify them as separate species. In some instances however they are identical and the little pink twin-flowered *Linnea borealis* for example, which was named after Linnaeus, the great botanist, grows right round the world in the northern temperate zone. Many European wild flowers have also become naturalized in North America since the European settlers arrived, and are now so widespread that it is often difficult to tell that they are not indigenous. One of these is the showy purple loosestrife, *Lythrum salicaria*, a European plant, which makes quite an impact in damp places along the eastern sea-board from Canada right down to Delaware.

North America is noted for some of the beautiful members of the lily family found there. These include the tall, graceful and very variable *Lilium canadense*, which grows in swampy places along rivers and streams, and the orange *Lilium philadelphicum* which prefers dry hilltops. The exciting golden yellow *Erythronium grandiflorum,* known as the glacier lily, and its relative the white avalanche lily, *E. montanum,* appear as soon as the snow melts in the western mountains, like crocuses do in the Alps. The strange green-flowered *Verartrum viride* is a medicinal plant of woodland glades and the various *Camassia* species, whose flowers range from white to purple, have edible bulbs.

Many of the wild flowers of the temperate regions of North America have come to enrich the gardens of Europe, and among them are several beautiful members of the evening primrose family. *Oenothera missouriensis*, a low, almost creeping plant of dry regions, is known as the glade lily, but this common name has not crossed the Atlantic to Europe. Both clarkias and godetias are American natives and so is the bergamot and the gay gaillardia, whose red and yellow flowers caused it to be known as fire wheel or Indian blanket. The best of the trilliums or wake robins are also American and the native species of golden rod and Michaelmas daisies, phlox, heleniums, rud-

beckias and the spiderwort, which are widespread throughout large areas of both Canada and the USA, have contributed enormously to the gay appearance of English herbaceous borders.

The autumn colouring of American woodlands is famous and among the many shrubs and trees which contribute to the splendour of the Fall are several kinds of dogwood, notably *Cornus nuttallii* and *Cornus florida.* These also have a spring display of large white or rosy red bracts surrounding clusters of small greenish-yellow flowers. The diervillas and the flowering currant, the false acacias, including the beautiful rose acacia, the pretty white flowered shad bush and the catalpa or Indian bean tree are all American shrubs and trees. The swamp rose and the prairie rose bear a close resemblance to the wild dog rose of Europe, but have rather darker flowers.

Both the vast grass prairies and the arid desert regions to the west have a character all their own, very different from the rest of the North American continent. As the altitude increases the prairie becomes a high plateau and the grass gives way to the so-called sage brush, or rabbit bush. These are tough, drought-resisting shrubs mostly of the genus *Artemisia,* with grey-green or purplish-grey leaves and small yellow or brownish flowers. In Arizona and New Mexico cacti and other succulent plants begin to appear, and enormous areas of the Sonoran desert are covered in creosote bush (*Larrea divaricata*), which after the spring rains bursts out in bright yellow, twisted flowers. This shrub, which reaches five or six feet in height, has a strong resinous smell and is a host plant of the lac scale insect, whose excretions are collected and used not only as a glue or water-proofing material but also in Indian medicine. The ocotillo (*Fouquiera splendens*), is another Mexican desert shrub whose tall, green and thorny stems carry tufts of scarlet flowers in early spring. The tiny leaves only appear for short periods after rain.

The agaves, magueys, or century plants, are typical of south-western North America. Over three hundred different species are known and most of them are native to Mexico. It is a myth that they only come into bloom once in a hundred years, although it is true that most agaves die after flowering. The age at which they flower depends on the climate and the soil, as well as on the species, but it may be anything from eight or nine years to 20 years, but seldom longer. An agave 50 years old

would be unusually ancient. The flower stalk, except in the very small species, is always tall and may either be branched like a candelabrum as in *Agave americana*, which is so familiar round the Mediterranean, or it may be a single spike as in *Agave utahensis*. The rather small flowers are either yellow or white, but occasionally dark red. Many agaves furnish fibres as well as sap, which is either used fresh as *aguamiel*, or fermented to produce alcoholic drinks like pulque or mezcal.

The yuccas have a much longer life than agaves and some of the woody species, which grow 20 feet or so in height at the rate of only an inch a year, may well be two or three hundred years old. There are only about 40 different kinds, and all of them have creamy flowers and rather narrow pointed leaves. They too yield fibres as well as soap substances and the flowers are often eaten both raw and cooked.

The Mexican cactus desert is unique in the world. It displays innumerable cacti like the giant saguaros and organ-pipe cacti, numerous flat-pad opuntias and the tree or shrub-like chollas or Teddy-bear cacti. Many different barrel cacti and mammillarias are also found here, which vary in size from quite tiny prickly balls to gruesomely spiny and massive plants as tall as a man. These huge old 'barrels' are known as compass plants, because they are always tilted towards the south west and so give some guidance to travellers trying to make their way through the desert, as well as providing an emergency supply of liquid.

Among the more gentle flowers of Mexico are the dahlias, the colourful zinnias, and the red cardinal sage, *Salvia fulgens*. The brightly spotted tigridia and the creamy-white zephyr lily (*Zephyranthes longifolia*) are two other natives, and there is a charming little annual (*Baileya multiradiata*) known as the desert marigold or paper daisy, whose golden flowers more or less dominate the desert landscape during the summer season.

Left

Matilija poppy *Romneya coulteri* Family
Papaveraceae
This Californian flower with its finely
pleated snow-white petals and the big
golden boss of stamens is even more
beautiful than the brilliantly coloured
oriental poppies which are more familiar
in Europe as garden plants. The blue-
green foliage sets off the flowers to
perfection and they remain open for
several days. It is a perennial, grows about
four feet high and is found wild in coastal
areas and in some of the canyons in the
Santa Ana Mountains. It resents root
disturbance and can only be transplanted
when young.

Below

Calico bush or **Mountain laurel** *Kalmia
latifolia* Family Ericaceae
Pink calico has gone out of fashion but
this enchanting North American evergreen shrub, with its clusters of parasol-
shaped flowers, is still considered a
beauty. The curved stamens form the
spokes of the parasol and the anthers are

at first tucked into pocket-like folds in
the petals. When bumble bees and other
insects blunder into the flowers seeking
honey, the stamens spring up towards the
centre, dusting their furry bodies with
pollen. The kalmia was named after Pehr
Kalm, a Finnish botanist who travelled in
North America in the middle of the
eighteenth century.

Right

Adam's needle *Yucca whipplei* Family
Agavaceae
Yuccas are very typical of the southern
States and Mexico and they are also
found wild in the West Indies, growing in
rather dry localities. Unlike agaves,
yuccas flower regularly and the plants do
not die after producing their spikes. The
large flowers are half closed in daylight
but at night they open fully to allow
Pronuba moths to enter and gather
pollen. These moths then fly on to other
flowers where they lay their eggs,
deliberately spreading the pollen to
ensure the development of the seeds on
which their caterpillars feed.

Left
Shooting star *Dodecatheon pauciflora*
Family Primulaceae
Except for the protruding anthers, the flowers of the shooting star are very like those of a cyclamen in shape. There are about fifty different species, all of them native to North America. They range from Alaska right down to California and are found in the eastern States as well. Most of the plants have flowers which are purplish or mauve, occasionally crimson or white, with a yellow edge to the coralla tube. They vary in size and leaf shape and the number of flowers borne on the stalk, which in the taller species may reach a height of two feet or so. These are woodland plants, preferring a semi-shady position.

Below left
Beard tongue *Pentstemon rupicola*
Family Scrophulariaceae
There are about 250 different Pentstemons and all but one, which grows in Russian Asia, are natives of the United States. They range from creeping mat-forming shrubs to small bushes and quite tall herbaceous plants, and are often so floriferous that the leaves are almost hidden when they are in full bloom. The flowers are more or less tubular, often with a prominent lip. Many of the species are excellent garden plants, although not always quite hardy in Britain, and there are also a great number of garden hybrids.

Top right
Lewisia tweedyi Family Portulacaceae
All the Lewisias are indigenous to North America and twenty or so different species are found among the mountains of the West, where they grow in rock crevices and in well-drained stony ground. *L. tweedyi* grows on Mount Stuart in the State of Washington and has larger flowers than most of the others. It makes a beautiful rock garden or alpine house plant and has a thick tuberous root. One member of the group, *L. rediviva*, was used as a food plant by the Red Indians, although its roots have a strong bitter taste. None of the Lewisias will tolerate lime so they must be grown in neutral or acid soil.

Right
Blue-eyed grass *Sisyrinchium bermudianum* Family Iridaceae
Sisyrinchiums are found both in North and South America in a hundred different forms. The pretty blue-eyed grass grows wild in the woods of the eastern States, from Florida up to Quebec in Canada and is also found on the islands of Bermuda and in western Ireland. It is a popular garden plant and quite easy to cultivate. The prairie blue-eyed grass, *Sisyrinchium campestre* is a native of the central North American plains where it grows among the grasses in full sunlight. It is taller than the previous species and the flowers are of a clearer blue.

Above
Magnolia *Magnolia grandiflora* Family
Magnoliaceae
The magnolias are a very ancient group of
plants, and fossil deposits show that some
five million years ago they were more
widespread than they are now. The most
splendid of the evergreen species is this
American magnolia whose large glossy
leaves are a rusty brown on the underside.
The huge white flowers, measuring eight
inches across, have a lemon scent and are
the floral emblem of Louisiana and
Mississippi. The tree grows wild in damp,
rich soil right across the southern States.
It needs a warm climate and although it
can be grown out of doors in southern
England it is usually planted against a
wall for protection.

Top right
Poinsettia *Euphorbia pulcherrima* Family
Euphorbiaceae
There are over 2,000 kinds of Euphorbia
scattered throughout the world, varying
tremendously in appearance from spiny

cactus-like plants, to shrubs and quite
small herbaceous species. The poinsettia,
a native of Mexico and very familiar as a
decorative plant, is grown in quantity for
the Christmas trade. The scarlet leaves are
not petals but only coloured bracts
surrounding the cluster of small greenish
yellow flowers. The poinsettia can only
be grown out of doors in tropical climates
and in the West Indies it is used as a
hedge plant. Like most Euphorbias it
contains a milky latex, which oozes out if
the stems are cut.

Right
Indian paintbrush *Castilleja miniata*
Family Scrophulariaceae
These interesting plants are found over a
wide area of North America, especially in
the west, and mainly in open country
among grasses. They have green leaves, but
are nevertheless semi-parasites which derive
extra nourishment from the grass roots.
The 'paintbrushes' are single stemmed,
and the bright colouring is not derived
from the flowers but from the bracts and

upper leaves, which make the plants very
conspicuous. The flowers themselves are
usually yellow or greenish and the colour
of the bracts varies in the different
species. Because of their parasitic habit
they are very seldom grown in gardens.

Far right
Hedgehog cactus *Echinocereus
engelmanni* Family Cactaceae
The cactus family comprises some 2,000
species, most of them natives of the arid
desert regions of Mexico, Arizona and
southern California. These plants have a
remarkable ability to survive drought by
storing water in the tissues of their
leafless stems and they are protected
against grazing animals by their fierce
spines. The plants themselves are ugly and
forbidding, but when the flowers are
produced they are often large and
beautiful. In some cases the flowers last
only for a single day or night, but other
species open their blooms for several days
in succession, closing them in the evening
at sunset.

South America

The tropical regions of South America contain a greater number of beautiful flowering plants than any other part of the world. These are still economically backward areas, where the original vegetation remains to a great extent unspoilt, and the soil and climate combine to produce exuberant growth. Trees, climbers and herbaceous plants reach their full stature more quickly than in most other parts of the world, and their number and variety is astonishing. These tropical forests are especially rich in lianas and climbers and although some of them have become quite familiar garden plants in many other parts of the world, the majority are still virtually unknown except to botanists who specialize in South American plants. For example the rosy-flowered *Mandevilla splendens* from the mountain areas near Rio de Janeiro, and the Chilean jasmine, *Mandevilla laxa*, were introduced to Europe in the first half of the nineteenth century, but there are over a hundred other members of the same genus which remain in obscurity. Pollination by bats or birds is quite a common phenomenon among plants in tropical South America. *Cobaea scandens* from Colombia, often known as temple bells, is a very rapidly growing climber with green or purple flowers and is cultivated in English gardens as an annual. Its faintly unpleasant smell attracts bats, who transfer the pollen on their furry bodies from one flower to another. The tiny humming-bird also performs the same service to many plants whose nectar-rich, often tubular flowers, attract them. Most of the hundred South American fuchsias are pollinated in this way.

The Bromeliads which include the pineapple family, are all of South American origin and a large number have become popular house and greenhouse plants. They vary a great deal in appearance and size, the largest and most extraordinary being the puyas which grow in the Andes. Immature plants consist of a thick round bunch of narrow, spiky leaves on top of a stout short trunk, but when the plants come into flower a tremendously tall spike develops from the centre of the crown. This sometimes reaches twenty feet or more in height and carries thousands of close-packed flowers, which may be greenish-white, blue or yellow. The leaves begin to droop, and when flowering is finished the plants die exhausted. The flowers produce abundant nectar which attracts birds as well as insects. One species, *Puya berteroniana*, has spiky shoots which grow out of the thick flower clusters to provide convenient perches for bird visitors that are unable to hover like the humming-birds.

Most of the Bromeliads have no stems, but consist of a rosette of stiff leaves, which are often spiny at the edges. In the epiphytic species these leaves form a kind of urn which collects water, and also acts as a trap for insects or small animals which are dissolved and absorbed. The leaves are often beautifully striped or coloured in red and yellow and the flower spikes have coloured bracts which contrast with the often rather small but bright flowers. In the pineapple, *Ananas comosus*, the flower cluster looks very like a huge pine cone and as the fruits ripen the bracts and ovaries fuse to form the juicy flesh. Pineapples are now grown in many parts of the world but the biggest plantations are in Hawaii.

The epiphytic orchids that grow on the forest trees in tropical America are famous and have been eagerly sought by collectors since the end of the eighteenth century. Perhaps the most famous of them all are the cattleyas, whose enormous pink and purple flowers are the most flamboyant of all the orchids. There are over 60 different wild species and any amount of cultivated hybrids. Other South American orchids include the strangely spotted odontoglossums, with many flowers on each spike, the pansy-flowered miltonias and the commercially important vanilla orchid, *Vanilla planifolia*, which is a climbing plant from tropical Mexico. The flavouring is derived from the seed pods, and was first used by the Aztecs in their chocolate drinks. The non-spiny cacti, like the Christmas cactus and the *Epiphyllum* and *Rhipsalis* species, also grow like the orchids on trees in the dense forests.

A number of popular garden plants which can be grown out of doors in Europe and North America, at least during the summer season, came originally from South America. The exotic looking canna, with red or yellow flowers, is a native of Brazil where it is found in boggy places. Its scientific name, *Canna indica*, is misleading but it has been introduced and naturalized both in Africa and parts of Asia. *Begonia semperflorens*, the ancestor of the popular summer bedding varieties, is another Brazilian plant, and the first tuberous rooted begonias, which had single flowers, came from Bolivia and the Andes. It was only in cultivation that they developed the heavy double flowers which we now know. All the begonias carry separate male and female flowers and many of them have decorative leaves.

The calceolarias, with their strange inflated blooms, grow

right across the continent from Mexico in the north to Patagonia in the south. There are about 400 different kinds ranging from quite large shrubs to tiny herbaceous plants. The size of the individual flowers tends to increase as the plants become smaller. For example the flowers on the shrubby specimens may measure less than half an inch across, but the tiny *Calceolaria darwinii*, which grows along the Straits of Magellan and stands only two inches high, bears solitary flowers an inch and a quarter wide. This strange little plant is hardy in southern England.

The attractive annual *Salpiglossis*, with large veined flowers, is a native of Chile and so are many of the verbenas. The scarlet *Verbena peruviana* grows on the Argentine pampas as well as in Peru. The glorious blue dawn flower, *Ipomaea learii* was introduced from South America and so was the morning glory, *I. purpurea* and *I. tricolor*, whose white buds are streaked with red, but open a rich blue. The climbing bougainvilleas also hail from there and are now grown in gardens all over the world,

wherever the winters are mild enough for them to survive. Their rich colouring comes from the bracts and not from the flowers.

Among outstanding South American plants that deserve a mention is *Cochliostema jacobianum*, an epiphytic plant which only occurs in Equador. It is not an orchid although its scented blue and mauve flowers have an orchid-like quality but belongs to the family Commelinaceae, which includes the many popular *Tradescantia* species. The wide strap-shaped leaves can reach four feet in length and several twelve-inch flower spikes appear at the same time. Europeans were amazed at the beauty of the plant when it was shown for the first time at the Paris exhibition in 1867. Another interesting plant is the giant water lily of the Amazon basin, *Victoria amazonica*, which can develop from seed to its full flowering size, with circular leaves six feet across, in a matter of seven months. It has eight-inch flowers, which open one at a time, and the stems may be eighteen feet long. It was first grown in the tropical house at Kew Gardens in 1846.

Below
Caiophora coronata Family Loasaceae
All the sixty-five species of *Caiophora* are
South American natives and this rather
appealing white-flowered species is a
mountain plant. It is found among rocks
and on scree in central Chile, usually at a
height between 8,000 and 10,000 feet.
The rough leaves are furnished with
stinging hairs, and although contact with
them is not as painful as with the
common stinging nettle, they are
certainly unpleasant to handle.

Bottom
Phrygilanthus mutabilis Family
Loranthaceae
This rather strange plant has flowers that
gradually change their colour from yellow
to red as they age. It is a semi-parasite on
Nothofagus, a South American tree
known as the southern beech. Like
its host, the parasite is evergreen and
therefore capable of manufacturing part
of its nutritional needs in its own leaves.

The genus includes 39 other species, some
of them totally leafless. One of these, *P.
aphyllus*, attacks the tree cactus *Cereus
chilensis*, and its red flowers erupt
directly from the stem of the cactus, as if
they were its own blooms. The mistletoe
is a member of the same family.

Right
Nasturtium *Tropaeolum polyphyllum*
Family Tropaeolaceae
All the members of this family come
from South America and there are
altogether some 80 different nasturtiums.
They grow mainly in mountain forests
and scrubland. Nearly all of them are
climbers and there are both annual and
perennial forms. *T. polyphyllum* has
deeply lobed leaves, unlike the common
nasturtium whose leaves are more or less
circular in outline. It flowers very
profusely, and is best planted at the edge
of a wall so that the swags of bloom can
hang down and be seen to advantage.

Left
Aechmea pineliana Family Bromeliaceae
Nearly all the members of the genus
Aechmea are epiphytes growing on forest
trees. Their stiff leaves form a hollow vase
which collects rain water and are
invariably furnished with small sharp
teeth along the edges. The flower spikes,
which rise singly from the centres of the
plants, have brightly coloured bracts,
which make a vivid contrast to the
flowers. Several species are popular pot
plants, including the one illustrated here,
and are grown commercially in large
quantities. One of the largest is *Aechmea
fulgens discolor* from Brazil, whose leaves
are purple on the under side.

Below left
Alstroemeria gayana Family
Alstroemeriaceae
This very attractive plant grows on the
sea shore in Chile. It belongs to the same
family as the climbing *Bomarea*, and the
same genus as the lily-like alstromerias
which are well known as garden plants.
Unlike most of the so-called Inca lilies it
is rather a low plant, with flower stems
seldom more than six inches tall. It has
the typical thickened leaves which are a
common feature of plants growing close
to the sea and which are subjected to
salty spray. The fleshy roots are
protected underneath the stones or in the
sand, and during the dormant season the
plant disappears from view.

Top right
Fuchsia *Fuchsia magellanica* Family
Onagraceae
This is the hardiest of all the fuchsias, and
is the parent of many improved garden
forms. It comes from the very southern-
most tip of South America where it grows
in the mountains of Magellan. It prefers
semi-shade and in the warmer parts of
Britain it makes a good hedge plant. In
colder areas it is normally cut to the
ground in winter but will survive and
grow up again in the spring. All fuchsias
make excellent pot plants and flower
continuously through the summer. There
are many other species in South America
and also several in New Zealand, but the
two groups will not hybridize although
they belong to the same genus.

Right
Brazilian coral tree *Erythrina crista gallii*
Family Leguminosae
This fine, showy shrub is indigenous to
Brazil and its waxy scarlet flowers appear
between July and September. The trunks
and branches are often rather spiny. It is
not fully hardy in Britain but can
sometimes be kept alive out of doors
against a warm wall, if the root is also
protected during the winter with a
covering of bracken and straw, but it will
not reach the size it does in warmer
climates. The genus includes some 170
different kinds of shrubs and trees, found
both in South America, tropical Asia and
South Africa.

Above
Passion flower *Passiflora antioquensis*
Family Passifloraceae
This beautiful climber from Colombia is
only one of the 400 different kinds of
passion flower. Most of them are found in
South America, but there are a few in
south-east Asia and Australia and also on
Madagascar. The first plants to reach
Europe were brought by the Spaniards
from South America, and it is likely that
the species was *Passiflora caerulea*, which
is now often grown as a pot plant. The
flowers are greenish white with a central
corona of red and blue filaments, five
greenish stamens and three prominent
nail-shaped stigmas. The strange
appearance of the flowers was interpreted
as symbolizing the crucifixion of Christ,
the stigmas representing the nails through
His hands and feet, the stamens His
wounds, the red inner corona the crown
of thorns, and the ten lobes of the flower
the faithful Apostles.

Above right
Chilean bellflowers *Lapageria rosea*
Family Philesiaceae

This outstandingly beautiful climber is
the floral emblem of Chile. It used to be
classified as a member of the lily family,
but is now grouped with only eight other
South American plants in a small and
exclusive family of their own. It is
reasonably hardy, so it is possible to grow
it out of doors in warm west country
gardens in Great Britain. It thrives in the
Scilly Isles where it flowers well. The
large, trumpet-shaped blooms have a
curious frosted appearance, as if the
petals were made of pink ice, dotted with
air bubbles. It is evergreen and prefers a
shady moist situation.

Top right
Fire bush *Embothrium lanceolatum*
Family Proteaceae
This beautiful shrub was found in the
Norquino valley in Chile by Mr H
Comber and well deserves its common
name. When it is in full bloom the flower
clusters clothe the branches completely in
scarlet so that the whole shrub appears to
be on fire. It is hardier than *Embothrium*

coccineum and can be grown successfully
in many parts of the British Isles, but it
must have soil which is free from lime
and rather moist. In Chile the fire bush is
often used as a hedge plant and grows
considerably larger than it does in
Europe.

Right
Bomarea caldesii Family
Alstroemeriaceae
There are over a hundred different
members of the genus *Bomarea*, all of
them natives of tropical America. They
are climbing or scrambling plants,
growing up through bushes and trees. *B.
caldasii* was discovered in Equador in
1802, where it grows quite commonly in
the mountains between 6,000 and 12,000
feet. The flowers are variable in colour,
and may be yellow or orange-red and
more or less spotted inside. Seeds did not
arrive in Britain until 1860 but since then
the plant has been grown in greenhouses
and also out of doors in mild localities,
especially in Ireland, where it is able to
overwinter safely.

Australia

Right
Morrison feather flower *Verticordia nitens* Family Myrtaceae
Endemic to Western Australia, the fifty *Verticordia* species are among the most unusual and charming of the Australian flowers. Their dainty, fluffy appearance is due to five heavily fringed calyx lobes which surround and set off the petals of the flowers. The colour may be white, pink, yellow, red or scarlet. In Australia they are often grown as garden plants and their general effect is not unlike that of massed Michaelmas daisies. Seed production is poor and germination uncertain, but cuttings will strike quite easily so there is no problem over propagation.

When Captain Cook reached Australia on his first voyage, the two botanists who had joined the expedition, Dr Solander and Joseph Banks, were amazed at the richness of the flora they discovered and gave the name Botany Bay to their main anchorage. They soon realized that many of the plants they found were quite unlike anything they had seen before, while even those which belonged to recognized botanical families were native species and unknown elsewhere.

Australia, New Zealand and Tasmania, although botanically in the same area, show considerable differences from each other. The climate ranges from tropical to temperate and the flora is as varied as the geography, which includes tropical rain forest, high mountains, fertile plains and vast stretches of arid desert country.

A great many of the Australian plants are specially adapted to withstand the rigours of a climate with long periods of drought. Most of the wattles for example do not have true leaves, but flattened leaf stalks instead which evaporate less moisture. Many other shrubs have either very small or thin needle-shaped leaves, and the foliage is often tough and leathery or covered in a woolly coating to prevent shrivelling.

The flowers are seldom large in size, but often very numerous. They produce a mass of pollen and plenty of nectar to attract bees, like the clustered blooms of the so-called bottle-brush shrubs and the extraordinary cylindrical flower heads of the banksias. Two other unique Australian plants are the Christmas bush whose flowers are white at first and then turn a clear red, and the yellow-flowered Christmas tree which belongs to the mistletoe family and is a root parasite, although it grows to tree size.

Of all the indigenous plants in Australia the grey-green eucalyptus trees or gums are the most typical and give the landscape its special character, while the acacias or wattles accentuate the sunshine with their fluffy yellow flowers clustered in tiny balls or elongated tassels.

Apart from the wattles, a great many other plants of the pea family (*Leguminosae*) are very common in Australia and appear in many different forms. One of the most vivid is Sturt's desert pea, *Clianthus formosus*, which grows in the dry interior of the continent, trailing over the ground and displaying its big red flowers which are marked with a raised black blotch. A close relative, the equally colourful parrot-bill or red kowhai (*Clianthus puniceus*), is a native of New Zealand and so is the yellow kowhai (*Sophora tetraptera*).

There are over a hundred different bush peas belonging to several separate genera, most of them carrying yellow, orange or brownish flowers. They take the place of the brooms of Europe and Asia and are particularly plentiful in Western Australia where they colour the landscape in spring. Several blue and purple bush peas, known as hoveas, are noted for their beauty. Among the trailing and climbing peas is the purple Kennedy pea, the rather sinister-looking black Kennedy pea and the red runner which often covers the ground like a carpet. The genus *Swainsonia* includes several twining peas, one of them being the dangerous darling poison pea which can be fatal to cattle and horses. Mount Rosea in the State of Victoria, received its name because during November and December it glows with the flowers of the rosy bush pea, a rare and local plant.

Many of the dry desert areas of Australia have very sparse vegetation, consisting largely of *Atriplex* species. This is known locally as salt bush, and it grows together with native grasses which have the ability to recover and grow again after long spells of drought. When rain does come these deserts can be transformed by masses of small annual flowers which spring up from seed. Several kinds of everlasting flowers are also native to Australia and grow in great profusion. Kangaroo paws are found in Western Australia and the red and green form has been adopted as the emblem of the state. These plants belong to the family Haemodoraceae and have hairy flowers which are gathered together in clusters. There are several different kinds, including the strange black kangaroo paw, whose flowers are yellowish-green inside.

In Queensland and the Northern Territory epiphytic orchids are found growing on forest trees. However the terrestrial kinds are far more numerous because the Australian climate is predominantly dry and in the west a great many fascinating orchids of the genus *Caladenia* occur. Many of them are blue, which is an unusual colour in orchids, and they carry surprisingly large flowers on very slender stalks.

Some of the strangest of the Australian plants are the various members of the genus *Xanthorrhoea*, known as grass trees or black boys. There are several different kinds and they all start off by looking like tufts of coarse grass. Gradually their trunks rise higher as the old leaves die away, and the base of the plant

is left bare with only a tuft of thick greyish leaves on top, looking like a huge head of untidy hair. Some kinds never grow more than two or three feet high while others, in old age, may reach twenty feet. An elongated spike of flowers springs from the centre of the leafy tuft. The individual flowers are quite small with protruding creamy white stamens, and they lie deeply embedded in protective chaffy bracts.

Two of the most important plant groups in New Zealand are the tree ferns and the manukas. These are shrubs of the genus *Leptospermum*, often referred to as tea trees because the early settlers in New Zealand used to brew a substitute tea from the leaves. The New Zealand flax, *Phormium tenax*, is another typical plant which belongs to the agave family. The long narrow leaves contain strong fibres which were used by the Maoris for weaving cloth and cord.

A great many New Zealand plants belong to the daisy family. The daisy bushes (*Olearia*) and the bush groundsels (*Senecio*) are numerous and many of these are now grown in gardens in Europe and America. Although Australia has many notable blue flowers, including the famous sky-blue leschenaultia, New Zealand strangely enough has no blue herbaceous flowers at all. There are a few yellow ones, but the great majority are white, including forget-me-nots, lobelias and some of the buttercups, and most of the interesting native alpines. One particularly strange New Zealand plant, *Raoulia eximia*, is known as the vegetable sheep because it forms huge mounds of densely packed woolly leaves which from a distance look just like resting sheep. Another little creeping plant with blue-green leaves, called the New Zealand burr (*Acaena novae zealandiae*) covers itself with brick-red spiny seed heads which are a great nuisance to the sheep farmers when they get tangled in fleeces. This plant is often grown in English gardens as a ground cover plant but does not appear to set fertile seed away from its native country.

Below
Beach lily *Crinum pedunculatum* Family
Amaryllidaceae
The crinums are tropical plants found in
many parts of the world and there are
half a dozen or so species which occur in
Australia and on some of the Pacific
Islands. This lovely white flower was
photographed on Lord Howe Island in
the south-west Pacific. The wide, tapering
leaves are dark green, and like all the
crinums it grows from a very large bulb.
It is nearly always found on beaches quite
close to the sea, and is spread from island
to island by its light, corky seeds, which
can float for long distances without
coming to harm in salt water.

Below right
Lobster claw *Clianthus puniceus* Family
Leguminosae
This striking shrub, with its curious
flowers reminiscent of red lobster claws,
is a native of the North Island of New
Zealand. The Maoris cultivated it long
before white men arrived on the scene
and called the shrub kowhai. It is also
known as the parrot-bill or the glory pea
and is now cultivated in gardens in many
parts of the world. It will even flower in
England in the mild south-western
counties, especially if it is trained against
a warm wall. It was first discovered in
New Zealand by the explorer William
Dampier, but was not introduced to
England until 1831. It is now virtually
extinct as a wild plant.

Right
Manuka *Leptospermum scoparium*
Family Myrtaceae
The tea trees or manukas are very
widespread in New Zealand and vary
tremendously in size and appearance. In
good soil they may grow up to twenty-
five feet in height, whereas in mountain
areas, in exposed positions and on poor
soil, they may be forced by circumstances
to creep along the ground. The flowers
are most commonly white, and when the
shrubs are in full bloom they look from a
distance rather like the hawthorn bushes
in England. Pink, or even rose-red forms
also occur, but are less common. They are
in no way related to the true tea tree, but
have been given this common name
because early settlers brewed a drink
from their leaves.

Below
Hebe speciosa hybrid 'Sapphire' Family
Scrophulariaceae
There are about 150 different species of
Hebe, all of them evergreen shrubs and
mostly native to New Zealand. They were
formerly classified as veronicas, but are
now considered to be a separate genus.
They vary considerably in size and
appearance, and some of them have only
very small leaves like scales which clasp
the stems. The small flowers may be
white, blue, violet, purple, pink or rosy
red and they are gathered together in
racemes, which are sometimes quite long
and very decorative. A great many
improved hybrids have been raised. They
can only be grown in mild climates, and
in Britain most of them are hardy by the
sea.

Below right
Chatham Island forget-me-not
Myosotidium hortensis Family
Boraginaceae
This beautiful plant, sometimes called the
Chatham Island lily, is found wild only
on this Pacific island about 500 miles east
of New Zealand. It once grew in
profusion along the sandy beaches, but
grazing sheep and rooting pigs completely
destroyed it in many places, so now it
only survives here and there in inacces-
sible places as a wild plant. The large,
deeply veined leaves act as funnels which
conduct rain water to the roots. It needs
a moist climate and an acid soil to thrive,
and has been grown successfully in
gardens not only in New Zealand but also
in Ireland and western Scotland where
this photograph was taken.

Right
Wattle or **mimosa** *Acacia cyanophylla*
Family Leguminosae
To be able to recognize and name all the
different Australian wattles would take a
lifetime of experience. There are nearly
600 different species, ranging from quite
low shrubs like the kangaroo thorn to
fair-sized trees like the blackwood. Most
of them have very small yellow flowers
which are gathered together in fluffy balls
or tassels, so that when a bush is in full
flower it looks completely yellow from a
distance. Many of the wattles have no
true leaves but merely flattened leaf
stalks or stems, which serve the same
purpose and are sometimes a beautiful
silvery colour.

Left
Albany banksia *Banksia coccinea* Family Proteaceae
The strange trees and shrubs are known as banksias in memory of Sir Joseph Banks, the English naturalist who accompanied Captain Cook on his first journey to the Pacific. They are found throughout Australia, but most of the fifty odd species are native to the western regions. They are often called honeysuckles, because their large cone-shaped flower heads provide an abundance of nectar for bees. The beauty of the flower heads, which are sometimes a foot tall, is due to the long styles which protrude from the closely packed, tiny flowers. The evergreen serrated leaves are frequently grey or brownish on the under surface.

Below
Borya septentrionalis Family Liliaceac
All the Borya species are entirely endemic to Australia. This one was photographed in its natural habitat on the Lamb's Head Mountain in Queensland where it grows at an altitude of 4,000 feet, in very shallow soil on top of rock. It is a member of the lily family, and is rather low and shrubby. The red colouring which is the main beauty of the plant is not derived from the flowers, but from the tufts of young leaves. The flowers, which are quite small and white and surrounded by dark bracts, are collected together in heads which stand up above the foliage.

Right
Beaufort myrtle *Beaufortia* Family Myrtaceae
This beautiful evergreen shrub was discovered in Western Australia and when it arrived in England in 1803 it was named after Mary Duchess of Beaufort. It needs a warm climate and cannot be grown out of doors in countries where there is a danger of winter frost. Botanically it stands fairly close to the *Callistemon* species, but the small, close-set leaves are rather reminiscent of heather. It is also known as the swamp bottle-brush and grows in open country on sandy soil which becomes very wet in winter.

Below right
Red-flowered gum *Eucalyptus ficifolia* Family Myrtaceae
This is the most colourful of the eucalyptus trees, but quite small in stature compared to the giants like *Eucalyptus regnans* which can grow 350 feet tall. There are about 500 different kinds of eucalyptus, most of them natives of Australia. When young, they carry very attractive juvenile foliage which is different from the mature trees. The flowers consist of a mass of stamens, and are usually white but occasionally yellow as in the yate, a tree noted for its tough wood. Many of the eucalypts provide valuable timber and during the nineteenth century blocks of their wood were used for paving the streets in London.

Blue Leschenaultia *Leschenaultia biloba*
Family Goodeniaceae
The fame of this brilliant blue flower has
spread far beyond its homeland in
Western Australia, and when it is in
bloom among the hills of the Darling

Range, people come from far and wide to
feast their eyes on its glorious colour. It is
a rather frail and delicate plant, classified
by botanists as a sub-shrub and has
narrow grey-green leaves, almost like
short spruce needles. Unfortunately it is

so temperamental that it is virtually
impossible to grow under cultivation, so
its beauty can only be enjoyed in places
where it still grows free and undisturbed.

Africa

With the exception of South Africa, the African continent as a whole is not noted for its flowers. It is characterized instead by the vast extent of certain kinds of rather monotonous types of vegetation, such as for example the savanna plains of central Africa, the bush veldt and the karoo of the south. Nearly half the continent north of the equator is occupied by the Sahara desert, the largest barren area in the world, and there are similar deserts on a smaller scale in south-west Africa, and in Somalia on the eastern coast. Equatorial rain forest and tropical forests cover less than a quarter of the continent, and the climate of the central African highlands is comparatively cool, although that area lies on the equator.

The high mountain vegetation is very interesting and unusual because of the peculiar conditions which prevail. Very strong sunlight and heat prevail during the day and frost during the night, and there is little seasonal change, so that no dormant period exists. Apart from the usual low and cushion-forming plants typical of mountain regions there are giant plants of *Lobelia* and *Senecio* species on several of the highest African mountains. They possess special adaptations to protect them from damage during a daily temperature fluctuation which may be as much as 18 degrees Centigrade. *Lobelia telekii* on Mount Kenya protects its growing point when young with its leaves, and later with a mass of long hairy bracts. The twelve feet tall *Lobelia deckenii* grows on Kilimanjaro in company with several different *Senecio* species. Among them is the rather low growing *Senecio brassica* whose woolly leaves, folded over the tender tip of the plant, look very much like a white cabbage. *Senecio keniodendron* grows up to eighteen feet in height, and while during the day its leaves spread out to catch the sunlight, at night they fold closely together to make a warm woolly coating for the stem, which protects it from freezing as the air temperature may drop to minus five degrees Centigrade.

The African forests contain many interesting trees with fine flowers, including the sausage tree, *Kilegia africana,* whose bat-pollinated blooms open at night. In arid sandy areas one finds the famous baobab, *Adansonia digitata,* with its swollen trunk and deciduous leaves shaped rather like those of a horse chestnut. The pendulous flowers with a huge boss of stamens are white and beautiful but have an unpleasant smell, and the fruits, like foot-long furry marrows are only relished by the baboons. The spectacular Flamboyant tree, with its brilliant red, orchid-like blooms, is not found wild in Africa itself, but is a native of Madagascar. Here it was discovered still growing wild in 1932 in a forest reserve on the west coast. It has been cultivated in SE Asia for a very long time and is now grown extensively in many other tropical countries.

Although Africa has no true lilies there are many other members of the lily family, notably the red-hot pokers (*Kniphofia*) and the aloes, of which there are over 300 species. In the plant communities of Africa aloes hold much the same place as the agaves do in America. Some cactus species have, unfortunately, been introduced to Africa and proved themselves to be a nuisance, but their native Old World counterparts, the euphorbias, have developed in Africa very much in the same way to resist heat and drought and may easily be mistaken for cacti when not in flower. Certain members of the milkweed family (*Asclepiadaceae*) also bear a remarkable resemblance to cacti, with swollen prickly stems. The most curious of all are the *Stapelia* species which have furry, mottled flowers which smell of carrion and attract quantities of flies which pollinate the blooms.

Among the many curious African plants which have found a way of surviving long periods of drought unharmed are the small 'stone plants' of the genus Lithops. When dormant these look exactly like mottled split pebbles and produce surprisingly large and colourful flowers from the fissure when the conditions are right. The welwitschia, a native of the Namib desert, and generally considered to be one of the ugliest and strangest plants in the world, is another of nature's freaks which can hang on to life under the most trying conditions for several hundred years. It produces only two leaves, which continue growing from the base throughout its life, even after the tips have withered and died. Although it is a flowering plant the fruits look like the cones of a conifer, and the great botanist Sir Joseph Hooker who studied the welwitschia in great detail considered it to be a missing link between the two.

Most of the beautiful flowers of Africa are found in the southern part of the continent, and especially in the region of the Cape of Good Hope, the homeland of the world-famous proteas. The Cape Peninsula alone, which is hardly larger than the Isle of Wight, has many more flowering plants than the whole of Britain. A great many of these are well suited to cultivation, not only in Africa but also in more temperate regions of

the world and have become well known and loved for their beauty and garden value. Most of the pelargoniums and geraniums which bring such cheerful summer colouring to window boxes and flower beds all over Europe and America have been developed from wild African ancestors, and so have the *Coleus* species, whose wonderful leaf colouring is so valuable for indoor and greenhouse displays. The saintpaulia, or african violet, is a native of Tanzania, and during this century has become one of the most popular of all the house plants, especially in the United States. The *Streptocarpus* species are also African in origin. One of the finest cultivars is constant nymph, which will flower for months on end in a cool greenhouse.

The ever popular busy lizzie (*Impatiens holstii*) and several other members of the same genus grow wild in tropical Africa, and both the so-called house linden, *Sparmannia africana*, an attractive indoor shrub with white flowers, and the sky-blue greenhouse climber *Plumbago capense*, were discovered in South Africa. Many of the finest daisy-flowered garden plants, both annuals and perennials such as *Venidium, Arctotis, Gazania, Dimorphoteca* and *Gerbera* species are South African wild flowers. So also are the colourful mesembryanthemums, including the hottentott fig which will grow on the south coast of Britain and is widely planted round the Mediterranean coasts.

Many other excellent plants have spread around the world from South Africa as garden flowers, pot plants or for use in the florist trade. The large sophisticated modern gladioli have smaller and more dainty ancestors in the Cape Province and the striking agapanthus with its huge umbels of blue flowers is another native. The pretty lachenalias, or Cape cowslips, are rather like yellow bluebells. They are not hardy, but the striking late autumn flowering *Nerine bowdenii* can be grown out of doors, at least in southern England. The amaryllis lily, the so-called Scarborough lily (*Vallota speciosa*), the *Clivia* and *Crinum Powellii*, are all African flowers of very high quality. The extremely long lasting chincherinche (*Ornithogalum thyrsoides*) is exported from South Africa as a cut flower to Europe, but it is a poisonous plant whose presence in grazing lands or in dried hay can cause the death of cattle and horses.

Another florist's flower from this region which has conquered the world is the arum lily, *Zantedeschia*. It grows in swampy places and in spite of its exotic appearance it is hardy also in Britain, especially if planted in water. In Australia it is now naturalized and threatening to become a weed. The rarer pink arum, which is a little smaller, is a native of Natal. The very beautiful and dainty South African heaths of the genus *Erica* are famous, and over 550 different species occur in the Cape Province. Unfortunately many of them have become very rare in the wild, and are restricted to single localities where they are now protected. The more common sorts are cultivated as pot plants and exported to Europe.

Left

African tulip *Spathodea campanulata*
Family Bignoniaceae
The brilliant scarlet flowers of this African
jungle tree always attract attention and it
is planted extensively in gardens and
parks for its ornamental value. The large
flowers are carried at the tips of the
branches in dense clusters and are
pollinated by birds and bats. The trees
grow about 60 feet high and the freshly
cut wood has an unpleasant smell of
garlic. In Tanzania and Kenya it is often
called flame of the forest and in some
African countries it is associated with
witchcraft.

Top right

Blood lily *Haemanthus multiflorus*
Family Amaryllidaceae
All the fifty members of this genus are at
home in tropical Africa. This specimen
was photographed close to the Victoria
falls, seen in the background of the
picture. It is a rainforest flower which
blooms only once a year with large heads
of tightly packed flowers and protruding
stamens. The strap-shaped leaves arising
from the large bulb remain at ground
level.

Right

Aloe *Aloe davyana* Family Liliaceae
This is quite a common plant of the
South African high veldt, where it flowers
during the chilly winter months. Most of
the 330 *Aloe* species are natives of Africa
and Madagascar and a few are also found
in Arabia. Many have been introduced as
garden plants to the Mediterranean
countries. They vary tremendously in
size, some being only a few inches high,
while others reach tree-like proportions.
The leaves are usually fleshy and rather
spiny and may be mottled or marked in
various ways. The flower spikes carry a
number of tubular flowers, and may be
either simple or branched. The flowers
themselves, although usually some shade
of pink or red, may also be white or
greenish or yellow.

Following page
Aeonium caespitosum Family
Crassulaceae
All the aeoniums have thick rosettes of
regular succulent leaves which are highly
decorative in themselves, and once a year
they produce large heads of densely
packed yellow flowers. They are found
both in North Africa and the Canary Isles
and are often grown as garden plants in
Spain, Portugal and southern Italy where
the climate is mild enough for them to
survive. Although they can withstand
prolonged drought, they are sensitive to
frost. In northern countries therefore
they must be grown under glass, although
they can be stood out of doors during the
summer.

Opposite Top left
Cleome luderitziana Family Cleomaceae
The cleomes are distributed all over the world in tropical and temperate regions and there are about 150 distinct species. Several of them have become specially adapted to desert regions by virtually dispensing with leaves, and this specimen was photographed in the Namib desert in South West Africa. The beautifully poised and coloured flowers are succeeded by long upright seed pods, very like those found in the family Cruciferae, to which they are fairly closely related. The pink or white spider flower, *Cleome spinosa,* is a native of South America, but is often grown in English gardens as an annual. In Europe the Cabbage White butterfly will select it as a food plant for its larvae.

Top right
King protea *Protea cynaroides* Family Proteaceae
More than a hundred different proteas are natives of South Africa and of these the king protea has the largest flower head, which can measure more than ten inches across. All the proteas are shrubs and the coloured leaves of the flowers are not petals but supporting bracts surrounding the cluster of small individual blooms in the centre. The evergreen leaves are rather tough and able to withstand long periods of drought. Cultivated proteas are grown in gardens all over South Africa and the king protea is the national flower. They have also been transplanted to parts of Australia, the Pacific coast of North America and to the Scilly Isles in Britain where they have become acclimatized and flourish.

Below left
Flame lily *Gloriosa simplex* Family Liliaceae
Although it belongs to the same botanical family as the aloes, this striking plant is totally different in habit and appearance. It is the national flower of Rhodesia and particularly interesting because it is the only liliaceous plant which is a climber. In the wild it scrambles over shrubs, clinging on with tendrils at the tips of its leaves. Although normally the flowers are red and yellow, at high altitudes they tend to be plain yellow. It is not hardy outside the tropics but is often grown elsewhere as a greenhouse plant. Five separate species are recognized which resemble each other closely.

Below right
Bird of paradise flower *Strelitzia reginae* Family Strelitziaceae
Few flowers are more strange and exotic looking than this South African native, which is also known as the crane flower because of its resemblance to a crowned crane. It grows wild along river banks and in open scrubland and is also now cultivated for the cut-flower trade in both Africa and America. The boat-shaped buds split along the top and the orange and dark-blue flowers emerge one by one over a period of days. They are pollinated by sunbirds and sugarbirds who transfer the pollen from flower to flower on their breast feathers. The Strelitzia family is closely related to the bananas, and the larger tree-like species are often called 'wild banana' in South Africa.

Above
Gold daisy *Gazania krebsiana* Family Compositae
The low growing gazanias are very typical of South Africa, and their brilliantly coloured flowers and silvery leaves make them very attractive garden plants for sunny climates. In northern countries they can be rather disappointing if there is a lack of sun, because the flowers will only open properly in sunshine. They have been in cultivation since the middle of the eighteenth century, and many beautiful hybrids have been raised with yellow, orange, red, white and brownish flowers with bands of contrasting colour round the central disc. They are only half-hardy in Britain and seldom survive the winter out of doors.

Top right
Geranium madarense Family Geraniaceae
Although the Canary Islands are geographically fairly close to Africa, their flora is quite distinct and more akin to that of the Mediterranean countries than to the neighbouring continental land mass. There are many endemic plants, found nowhere else in the world and among them is this very attractive and robust herbaceous geranium whose numerous pink flowers rise from a large rosette of spreading divided leaves. It has recently been introduced to English gardens, and will survive normal winters in the south. In Cornwall and on the Scilly Isles it is reliably hardy.

Right
Shimmering daisy *Dorotheanthus bellidiformis* Family Aizoaceae
Like the gazanias, these shining flowers respond to the sun and occur in many colours including purple and crimson. Seedsmen often list them under the name of *Mesembryanthemum criniflorum* and they are easily grown as half-hardy annual plants, which spread out more or less flat on the ground. The specimen in the picture was photographed in Namaqualand in South Africa where it is one of the common wild flowers. The leaves are thick and fleshy and able to withstand extremely hot and dry conditions. The very fine seeds are scattered by the wind.

Above
Milkweed *Pachycarpus schinzianus*
Family Asclepiadaceae
This is a spring flowering plant from the
Transvaal high veldt, and is one of thirty
allied species which all contain a milky
juice in their leaves and stems. The plant
grows about eighteen inches high. The
flowers are rather intricate and have
cup-shaped outer corolla surrounding
the smaller, coloured petals. They are
an inch and a half wide and are
pollinated by flies. Several other
members of the same family are very like
cacti in appearance.

Left
Flame gold-tips *Leucadendron discolor*
Family Proteaceae
These shrubs belong to the same family as
the proteas but carry male and female
flowers on separate plants. Those
pictured here are male and consist of a
large boss of red anthers which turn
yellow when the pollen is ripe. The
female flowers have green stigmas, and
the flowers are surrounded by petal-like
yellow bracts. The plant is a shrub,
reaching about six feet in height and it is
cultivated for its flowers, which last well
in water. All the Leucadendron species
need a warm climate and they are not
hardy in Britain except in the Scilly Isles.

Asia

Whether the Garden of Eden was a reality or just a myth, the fact remains that Asia has given to the world its most delicious fruits and many of its finest flowers. The ancient trade routes from China to India and Persia, Turkey and the eastern Mediterranean countries formed a line of communication right across the huge continent. Along this route seeds, plants and information on their culture gradually spread to the west, although it is now so long ago that nobody can prove it. We do know, however, that the apricot and the peach were originally grown in China, that the grape is almost certainly of Asiatic origin, and that apples, pears and plums were first cultivated there. The citrus fruits too are natives of south-east Asia, and the banana came from the islands between Asia and Australia.

The Asian countries west of India are mainly dry and rather barren areas, apart from the river valleys, but it is from here that many fine and colourful garden plants have been obtained. Wild tulips, fritillaries and anemones decorate the brown hills in spring, and *Cyclamen persicum*, the parent of the large-flowered greenhouse varieties, was collected here. The flaming oriental poppy is a native of Turkey and Iran, and so are a great many irises. These include the marvellously veined *Onocyclus* irises, whose beauty intrigued even the mighty Egyptian Pharaohs 2,000 years before the birth of Christ. Lilies, roses and almond trees were grown in Persian gardens many centuries before there were any proper gardens in Europe at all, and cultivated magnolia trees in China were already old and gnarled in the days of the Roman Empire.

The southern mountain ranges of the Himalayas are a treasure house of fine plants, but it was not really until the beginning of this century that plant hunters from the west were able to explore the area thoroughly. One of the most noted was George Forrest who made several expeditions before he died in the mountains. He was later followed by Frank Kingdon-Ward, who concentrated his attention on the mountains on the borders of Yunnan, China and Tibet.

The rhododendrons of these mountain ranges are extremely numerous and variable. They may be giants like the rose-pink *R. giganteum*, reaching 80 feet in height, or tiny creeping shrubs like the red *R. repens* and the curious *R. forrestii*, whose crimson bell-shaped flowers cling like ivy to the rocks. Many of the evergreen azaleas came from Japan, and the little *Azalea simsii*, which is the parent of the modern greenhouse azaleas, has been grown in Europe since early in the nineteenth century. The strongly scented yellow *Azalea pontica* is now known as *Rhododendron luteum* and came to western Europe from the Caucasus in 1793. *Rhododendron ponticum* came from the same area but had already arrived some twenty years earlier. It was thought at first that rhododendrons and azaleas were botanically distinct, but they are now all classified together as members of the genus *Rhododendron*. Innumerable garden forms and hybrids have been raised, using both Asiatic and American species as parents.

The high mountain slopes have yielded many fine plants including the autumn flowering gentian, *Gentiana sino-ornata*, whose intense rich blue rivals that of the *Alpine G. acaulis*. In the moist valleys and well-watered meadows grow many different primulas of coppery yellow, orange and white or with tiers of reddish-purple flowers. George Forrest brought many of these plants to Europe. He also discovered the dainty *Primula malacoides* in Yunnan, and was responsible for re-discovering the exotic-looking but perfectly hardy *Incarvillea delavayi*. This has large, rose-pink flowers, and had been lost to cultivation after it was first sent to France by Abbé Delavay. Several other French missionaries in China were also interested in plants and made many new discoveries. The butterfly bush, *Buddleia davidii* is named after Abbé David, and Père Giraldi was the first to find the pretty pink bush, *Kolkwitzia amabilis*, which is known in the USA as the beauty bush.

The Swedish botanist Carl Thunberg was the first to notice cultivated Japanese forms of *Hydrangea macrophylla* in the late 1870s. These became the parents of our present-day mob-cap and lace-cap hydrangeas, and other species were later found in China and Korea. The sweet-scented jasmine came originally from northern India and Persia. Its rich perfume was much appreciated and it reached Europe as early as the sixteenth century. The Persian lilac arrived about a hundred years later. The wistaria came from Japan in 1830, and in 1850 Robert Fortune found in China the large-flowered *Clematis lanuginosa,* which became the ancestor of many fine garden forms.

The Japanese countryside was at one time full of lilies, but once they became known in the west a commercial demand was created, and so many bulbs were dug up for sale that very few wild lilies now remain there. The most famous of the Japanese lilies is the golden-rayed lily, *Lilium auratum*, which has huge brown-spotted white flowers streaked with gold. Another of

their treasures is *Lilium speciosum*, which is spotted and flushed with crimson and has a powerful scent. The tiger lily has been cultivated in China, Japan and Korea since ancient times, not so much for its flowers as for the bulbs, which are edible. The regal lily, *Lilium regale*, is one of the world's top flowers but was not introduced to western gardeners until 1910, when the American plant hunter, E. H. Wilson, came upon it growing in great abundance in the Min valley, on the borders of China and Tibet. Several thousand bulbs were sent to America, and it is from this one consignment that all the regal lilies now in cultivation are descended.

The giant lily, *Cardiocrimum giganteum*, came from Yunnan. It grows over ten feet tall and has narrow trumpet-shaped white flowers a foot long. Nearly all the Hosta species are Japanese, and so are the excellent, trouble-free day lilies (*Hemerocallis*). The bergenias or bear's ears which make good ground cover arrived from central Asia. There are probably many interesting flowers still remaining undiscovered in remote parts of Mongolia.

The tropical regions of south-east Asia are of quite a different character. Here are the steamy green rain forests whose trees carry their flowers high up out of sight. One of the most remarkable of these, *Amsherstia nobilis*, is a native of south Burma, and has crimson and yellow flowers. *Cassia fistula*, often called the Indian laburnum, grows wild in the jungle, while another lovely deciduous tree with pink flowers, 'the queen of flowers', *Laegerstroemia speciosa* is found more often in open country.

South-east Asia is the home of many fine orchids, of the curious insect-trapping nepenthes, or the climbing hoyas with their waxy, scented flowers, and the beautiful blue climbing *Thunbergia grandiflora*. The ginger family, which includes about ninety different species, comes from here and so does the genus *Rafflesia*. These curious plants have no leaves at all and produce only strange fleshy flowers. The most famous is *Rafflesia arnoldii* from Sumatra, whose enormous red and cream-blotched flowers measure a yard across and sit flat on the ground.

Above

Anemone *Anemone coronaria* Family
Ranunculaceae
This lovely plant, with three-inch flowers
in scarlet, blue or purple, is a native of
the Middle East. In the Sermon on the
Mount the lilies of the field were
mentioned as being more gorgeously
arrayed than 'Solomon in all his glory'. In
fact they were probably these anemones,
which make such a wonderful show in
spring. Legend has it that they first
arrived in Europe as corms in the ballast
of ships returning to Pisa after taking the
Crusaders to the Holy Land. They have
certainly been long in cultivation and are
the ancestors of the modern St Brigid
and De Caen anemones.

Left

Sacred lotus *Nelumbo nucifera* Family
Nelumbonaceae
The pink-flowered lotus is as often
associated with the Nile that it has come
to be regarded by many as an Egyptian
flower, but its real homeland is India and
the Far East. It was probably introduced
to Egypt sometime in the sixth century
BC. It is esteemed as the sacred flower of
Buddha, and at the same time it is also a
plant of considerable economic
importance. It is cultivated for food and
both the seeds, leaves and rhizomes are
prepared and eaten in various ways. Even
the stamens are used for flavouring tea.

Right

Epiphytic orchid *Phalaenopsis amabilis*
Family Orchidaceae
Although it is not brightly coloured, this
beautiful gold and white orchid has all
the style and elegance that one associates
with these splendid flowers. Like most of
the large orchids it is an epiphyte,
growing in nature on the rough bark of
jungle trees, where its roots manage to
find enough nourishment through
symbiosis with certain fungi. The orchid
family is a very large one, with something
like 18,000 different species found all
over the world, and new ones are still
being discovered. They are very much
sought after as greenhouse plants and
innumerable hybrids and cultivars have
been raised.

Left

Indian Balsam *Impatience glandulifera*
Family Balsaminaceae
This stately annual from the Himalayas
is a water-side plant, which grows very
rapidly to a height of five feet or so and
flowers in late summer. Like all the
balsams it has stems which are so full of
water that they are more or less trans-
lucent, and as well as producing plenty
of nectar in its flowers, it also carries
nectar glands on the leaf stalks. This
plant was introduced to England in
1839 and now can be found along
streams and river banks all over the
country. When ripe, the seeds jump out
of the pods, scattering in all directions,
They are carried by the water down-
stream and so the flower is spread from
place to place.

Below left

Blue corydalis *Corydalis cashmeriana*
Family Fumariaceae
This delightful plant belongs to the same
family as the bleeding heart, and has a
similar delicate air. It hails from Kashmir
and needs a cool situation and moist,
peaty soil. Even when given these
conditions it does not always thrive and is
generally considered rather difficult to
grow. There are a number of corydalis
species, all of them with finely cut, soft
foliage. One of the yellow-flowered
forms. *Corydalis lutea,* is naturalized in
England and prefers to grow in crevices in
shady walls. It flowers almost perpetually
throughout the summer.

Right

Blue poppy *Meconopsis grandis* Family
Papaveraceae
When Frank Kingdon Ward discovered
the blue poppies in the Himalayas and
introduced them to England in 1924,
they aroused immediate interest and
admiration. The only European
Meconopsis is the yellow Welsh poppy
and these Asiatic species are much more
exciting. They are mainly blue in colour,
but also in some cases pale yellow or
purple. Unfortunately they tend to be
monocarpic, which means that they
flower only once and then die, so new
plants have to be raised from seed or
offsets. The intensity of the blue
colouring depends on the soil and climate
and they will not grow in chalk.

Above
Fox-tail lily *Eremurus robustus* Family
Liliaceae
These imposing plants carry their thick
trusses of bloom on stalks up to twelve
feet tall, and are found right across
central Asia from Turkey to western
China. The greatest concentration
however is in Afghanistan and in the
mountain areas in the south of the Soviet
Union. There are about fifty separate
species, with pink, white or yellow
flowers and they often grow in large
groups on the arid, stony slopes where
grazing flocks of sheep and goats have
eaten most of the other herbage. They are
related to the asphodels of southern
Europe and have similar strap-shaped
leaves.

Top right
Mucuna bennetti Family Leguminosae
A great many colourful creepers grow in
south-east Asia and this example from
New Guinea is one of the most brilliant.
The genus *Mucuna* includes over a
hundred different kinds, found both in
the Old and the New World. Another very
beautiful species is *Mucuna atropurpurea*,
a native of Ceylon and India. It carries
trusses of fine violet-purple flowers, and
the large seed pods which follow are
covered in short red hairs which later
drop off. It is unwise to handle the pods
while they are young and furry because
the hairs are poisonous and can cause
severe skin irritation.

Centre top
Wild rose *Rosa macrophylla* Family
Rosaceae
Asia is the home of a great number of
wild roses and many of them have
contributed to the breeding of present-
day garden varieties. *Rosa macrophylla* is
at home in northern India, Kashmir, the
Himalayas and western China. It is a
strong grower, reaching ten feet in height.
The stems are reddish in colour and the
bottle-shaped hips are bright scarlet and
rather bristly. It was introduced to
English gardens at the beginning of the
nineteenth century and was given an
Award of Merit by the Royal Horti-
cultural Society in 1897.

Far top right
Hibiscus *Hibiscus rosa-sinensis* Family
Malvaceae
The red hibiscus is now the national
flower of Malaysia although it originated
in China and is commonly grown in
tropical countries all over the world.
Many different varieties have been raised,
some of them with enormous flowers,
and the colours vary through many
shades of pink, red and yellow. They are
always characterized by a long stamen
tube with numerous yellow stamens and
red stigmas at the tip. The only kind of
hibiscus hardy in England is *Hibiscus
syriacus*, a shrub with much smaller
flowers than the Chinese species. The
tropical hibiscus can be successfully
cultivated as a pot plant in greenhouses.

Previous page
Rhododendron cinnabarinum Family
Ericaceae
The rhododendrons, in all their variety,
are undoubtedly the most striking
members of this family. The great
majority are natives of Asia, especially
the Himalayan region, but they are also
found in China and Burma. A few species
are natives of North America. One of the
most distinctive types is the *Cinnabarinum* species shown here, which is
indigenous to the state of Sikkim. These
rhododendrons are characterized by their
abundant narrow, tubular flowers which
are often tinged with yellow or orange.
The rounded evergreen leaves are of an
unusually attractive blue-green colour.

Above
Spurge *Euphorbia wallichii* Family
Euphorbiaceae
The herbaceous spurges which have
become very highly regarded as garden
plants in Britain since the 1950s, occur
in many different forms throughout
Europe and Asia. The flowers are
insignificant but surrounded by coloured
bracts, usually more or less yellow or
occasionally orange. Spurges cannot be
called conventionally beautiful, but they
have an arresting architectural quality
which sets them apart from other garden
plants. Some are evergreen, like the
creeping *Euphorbia myrsinites* and the
large *Euphorbia charachias* with its
enormous green flower trusses, while
others die down to ground level in winter.
Euphorbia wallichii is a native of
Kashmir.

The development of garden flowers

The appearance of a healthy flower is due to its inherited characteristics, and these are determined by the genes carried by the chromosomes in its cells. Each gene is responsible for a certain feature of the plant such as its flower colour, shape, size, the height of the plant, the texture of the leaves, the time of flowering and so on. Some genes are dominant over others, and when they are present the features governed by them will always appear, although there may be latent possibilities of different characteristics.

When cross-pollination takes place between two plants, the genes carried in the reproductive cells sometimes become re-arranged in the chromosomes, and by pure chance one chromosome may get a double amount of a normally recessive gene. A seedling carrying this chromosome in its cells would in such a case differ noticeably from its parents. It might grow unusually large, or have double flowers instead of single ones, or have petals of a different colour. In nature, odd freaks or so-called mutants like this are apt to disappear again, because unless they are self fertile or receive pollen from a similar freak plant, all their seedlings will revert to normal.

When plants are grown in gardens, new forms are immediately noticed. If they are better than their parents they will be cherished and isolated, and then deliberately bred or propagated from cuttings so as to perpetuate a new and desirable characteristic. Over the years the great majority of garden plants have been improved by selection, cross-breeding and hybridizing, and so new strains have been produced which have greater decorative value than the original wild forms. Gardeners today owe an immense debt to the Chinese, because it was they who began developing flower growing as an art many centuries before anybody else. When the chrysanthemum, the paeony and the camellia arrived in the West, they were already very sophisticated plants which had been bred for so many years that a large number of different varieties had been obtained.

Cultivation of the chrysanthemum in China goes back nearly 25 centuries to 500 BC. The garden chrysanthemum is a hybrid, whether deliberately produced or accidental it is not possible to say. However its two ancestors were most likely the yellow *Chrysanthemum indicum* and *Chrysanthemum morifolium* which has either white or purple flowers. Their progeny has been named *Chrysanthemum hortorum*, which makes it quite clear that it is a garden plant, and in the skilled hands of gardeners, both in China and later on in Japan, it has given rise to an apparently endless succession of new forms, which are still being improved. This universally popular flower has only been grown in Europe since 1789, but became a favourite so quickly that fifty years after its introduction, over a hundred different varieties were already being grown in England. It can now be brought into bloom all through the year.

The paeony occurs wild in Europe and in many parts of Asia, including Siberia, but once again it was the Chinese who first appreciated it as a garden flower and began to select and breed it. The wild white Asiatic paeony, *Paeonia lactiflora*, was first mentioned in Chinese literature during the 5th century BC, and a few hundred years later the tree paeony or moutan also came into fashion in China where it was cultivated to high perfection. The yellow form was especially sought after, and high prices were paid for plants or even for single flowers. The western nations lagged far behind and did not begin to develop paeonies until the eighteenth century when the first few Asiatic plants were imported.

The ancestry of garden roses is now impossible to unravel but we do know for certain that one of the forebears was *Rosa gallica*. It is likely that this red rose was brought into Europe by the Persians who had been keen rose growers for hundreds of years before they invaded the west. It was the semi-double form of *Rosa gallica* which was later chosen as an emblem by the house of Lancaster, while the white rose of York was *Rosa alba*, a very old hybrid whose parentage is unknown. *Rosa moschata* is an autumn flowering white rose whose modern descendants are known as musk roses. *Rosa moschata* now seems to have disappeared in the wild, but it too was grown in ancient Persia, so its homeland was probably somewhere in the Middle East.

The early roses bred in Europe all had a comparatively brief flowering season. The long flowering habit of modern roses was derived from a mutation of the Chinese rose, *Rosa chinensis*. In its original wild form this was a climbing rose with a short season. In cultivation it produced a sport, which was a shrub instead of a climber, and which flowered continually through the summer. It came to Europe, probably by way of Persia, in the sixteenth century. Another freak rose which also first appeared in China was the tea rose, *Rosa gigantea*. The first variety of this to arrive in Europe was known as the pale China rose and it flowered for the first time in England in 1793. It was

the hybrids between these two sports which became the ancestors of the vast majority of modern garden roses. Serious European rose breeding first started in France and many roses still bear French names. The Empress Josephine, Napoleon's first wife, established a large collection of roses at Malmaison. Although the so-called old-fashioned roses are not as floriferous over a long period as the modern varieties, they have such a charming scent and are so lovely that many discerning gardeners still appreciate them.

The development of the modern garden lupin from wild American species is a story of the present century that was only completed just before the second world war. The man who brought all the gorgeous colours and combinations of colour into lupins was George Russell, an Englishman, and it took him twenty-five years to achieve what he wanted. He did not use deliberate hand-pollinating methods, but simply planted *Lupinus polyphyllus*, which has blue, white and pink forms, in close proximity to the yellow tree lupins, also including in his collection some colourful annual Mexican species. Wild bees did the rest and every year when his latest crop of seedlings flowered, George Russell ruthlessly destroyed all plants which did not show an improvement or a new colour combination. The good plants were retained, and this process went on year after year with only very gradual improvement. Fifteen years after he had begun his work there was a sudden leap forward with new and spectacular colour breaks appearing, and from then on the annual improvement of the strain became very noticeable. In 1937 when these lupins were first exhibited to the public they caused a sensation, and their glorious rainbow colourings put all other lupins in the shade. Russell lupins have now completely replaced all the older strains and although they do not come true from seed, the best named varieties are propagated commercially from cuttings.

Above
Delphinium Family Ranunculaceae
No other plants can really rival the large
delphiniums for stately beauty, but they
are demanding plants to grow, and need a
deep rich soil and secure staking to give
of their best. Delphiniums have been in
cultivation since the days of ancient
Egypt and it is not known for certain
how the early garden forms were derived.
They undoubtedly have Asiatic
parentage, although wild species are
found also in North America and in
Africa. Most of the wild delphiniums are
some shade of blue or violet, but there
are also four yellow species including *D.
zalil* from Persia and two scarlet ones, *D.
nudicaule* and *D. cardinale* in California.
Many of the wild blue delphiniums
produce white forms from time to time,
especially *D. formasanum* from the
Caucasus. The massive compact spikes of
modern delphiniums are the result of
years of painstaking breeding and
selection. The attempts during this
century to bring in the red colouring
from the Californian species has proved
especially difficult, even when seedlings
have been treated with colchicine to

overcome problems of sterility. Most of
this work has been done by Dr R A Legro
of Wageningen in Holland and by 1962 he
had succeeded in producing large flowered
delphiniums in many shades of red,
yellow and orange. He then went on to
try and introduce the strong scent of the
white African *Delphinium leroyi* with
considerable success. There is little doubt
that large, scented delphiniums in a big
range of colours will be generally
available to gardeners well before the end
of this century.

Right
Dahlia Family Compositae
The Mexican dahlias were already
improved garden plants when Vincente
Cervantes, who was in charge of the
botanic garden in Mexico City, first sent
them in the form of seeds to his friend
Abbé Cavanilles in Madrid in 1789. They
were intended to be used for food, rather
in the manner of potatoes, but few
people liked the flavour of the tubers.
The dahlia would then probably have
been completely neglected in Europe if
the Empress Josephine had not taken a
fancy to the flowers and started to grow

them in her garden at Malmaison. Since
that time dahlias have undergone such a
change that neither the Abbé Cavanilles,
nor the Swedish botanist Andreas Dahl
after whom they were named, could
recognize them any longer. From being a
vegetable, the dahlia has become the
queen of the late summer flower garden
in all its colourful variety and a favourite
for the show bench.

Far right
'Peace' Family Rosaceae
Many people think that 'Peace' is the
greatest rose of this century. It was raised
by F Meilland at his rose nursery on Cap
Antibes in the South of France and
received its first Gold Medal in the USA
in 1944, followed by four more top-class
awards in the next three years. It is an
exceptionally vigorous and healthy rose
which should not be hard pruned. The
flowers are large and full, but their
delicate colouring saves them from
looking heavy and they stand up well to
bad weather. It is not powerfully scented,
but its many other good qualities make
up for this.

Below right
Carnations and pinks Family
Caryophyllaceae
Dianthus caryophyllus, the ancestor of
the carnation, is a rather small wild
flower native to southern Europe and the
Near East. It has also been naturalized in
many parts of France including
Normandy, as well as on old walls in
England. The clove carnation is one of
the really old garden flowers and has been
cultivated in Europe for at least 2,000
years and probably longer than that in
the East. The Greeks referred to it as the
divine flower and in England, where it
probably arrived with the Normans, it
became known as sops in wine, or
gilliflower. This is probably a derivation
from the French *geillet oiroflée*. In
Germany and Holland the flower is
known as *Nelke* and in Sweden it is called
nejlika. The Dutch painter Jan van
Eyck's famous portrait 'The man with the
carnation' painted about 1430, shows a
serious looking gentleman in a fur hat and
silver chain with cross and bell, holding a
small red and white carnation in his right
hand. The striping or mottling appeared
quite early in cultivated carnations, and
when the great Dutch flower painters
depicted them in their splendid pictures
they had become very much larger and
more varied in colour. Carnation shows
were held in Elizabethan times, but it was
not until the beginning of the nineteenth
century that the custom of improving the
appearance of the flowers by 'dressing'
began. Appropriately enough it was
started by a hairdresser named Kit Nunn,
and now competitors dress not only their
carnations but their chrysanthemums as
well as a matter of course, using much the
same technique as is employed in
arranging curls of hair. The first long-
flowering carnations were raised in
Europe in 1750 and became known as
remontants, but did not arouse much
interest elsewhere until American
breeders took over. They raised many
new varieties including the famous Mrs S
Lawson, a pure pink flower which
became the parent of many later
cultivars. The carnation illustrated here is
one of the so-called border carnations
which can be grown successfully out of
doors in Britain, and flowers for most of
the summer.
Pinks have smaller flowers and form
much more branching and compact plants
than carnations proper. They are
descended from *Dianthus plumarius*,
another pink-flowered wild plant with the
same distribution as *D. caryophyllus*. The
most famous of them all is the strongly
scented, snow-white double pink called
Mrs Sinkins, which first appeared in the
workhouse garden at Slough in about
1870 and was named after the master's
wife. It is still grown in many gardens
today.

Above
Bearded iris Family Iridaceae
The most widely grown and beautiful of
all the cultivated irises are the tall
bearded forms which have a wider range
of colouring than almost any other
garden flowers. They are not, as is often
said, descendants of the European *Iris
germanica*, for it is a sterile plant. In fact
they have arisen from hybrids between
Iris pallida and *Iris variegata*, both of
which are found round the Adriatic and
even hybridize in the wild. The first
growers to start selecting seedlings of
these irises at the beginning of the
nineteenth century were a German, E von
Berg, and a Frenchman named de Bure.
They were followed by others, notably M
Lemon who continued to produce new
cultivars steadily for more than fifteen
years. Later on several English nursery-
men like Peter Barr and Amos Perry also
took up iris breeding. New varieties are
still being raised and their popularity as
garden plants continues. All these irises
need good drainage and sunlight, and
prefer a soil which is alkaline.

Right
Hybrid lilies Family Liliaceae
The wild lily species are such beautiful
plants that the idea of improving them
still further did not arouse much interest
until the beginning of this century. One
of the first lily breeders was Mrs R O
Backhouse, who crossed *Lilium hansonii*
with *L. martagon* to produce the
Backhouse hybrids in the 1890s. North
American lilies played a large part in the
breeding of the vigorous turk's cap type
Bellingham hybrids which appeared in the
1930s and in recent years the most
spectacular lilies have been the result of
work done by Jan de Graaff in Oregon.
His magnificent yellow trumpet lilies
have been especially admired. The most
famous of these was golden clarion, but
many more have followed, including
honeydew which is illustrated here. The
hybrid lilies are often easier to grow than
many of the species, but they are also
unfortunately very susceptible to virus
disease. However it is possible that this
tendency can be overcome by further
breeding from resistant species.

Following page
Tulip Family Liliaceae
The rather stiff appearance of the tulip
has always appealed to tidy gardeners, and
the Dutch with their sense of order and
preference for formal gardens, were just
the right people to welcome and cherish
this Turkish flower when it first reached
Europe in 1554. Tulips were soon
springing up in new forms and colours in
the flat fertile fields of Holland and by
1634 people were in the grip of
tulipomania. They used to spend
ridiculous sums on single bulbs of new
varieties, but in time the craze died down.
Tulips are still grown in vast quantities
though, and since the second world war
many previously unknown tulip species,
with attractively patterned leaves, have
been brought into cultivation.

Acknowledgments

The publishers would like to thank the following organizations and individuals for their kind permission to reproduce the pictures in this book:

H R Allen, NHPA 20 top, 26, 42 right, 55 top, 56 bottom, 67 top
Australia House 11 bottom
A-Z Collection 36 top, 37 top, 53 bottom left, 66, 68 right, 69 below left, 69 right, 70, 71 bottom
Anthony Bannister, NHPA 13, 51 bottom, 53 top left
K Beckett, NHPA 11 top, 34 36 bottom
Ann Berry 54, 55 bottom, 56 top
R J Corbin, NHPA 38 right, 41, 48

Stephen Dalton, NHPA 60 top
Douglas Dickins, FRPS, NHPA 31 top 50, 53 bottom right
Eric Elms, NHPA jacket front flap, 46 bottom
Valerie Finnis, NHPA endpapers, 4-5, 15, 21 bottom, 28-30, 35, 37 bottom, 39, 44, 45 bottom, 60 bottom, 61, 62 left, 71 top 72
Ron Foord, NHPA 8 bottom
J Game, NHPA 42 left
David R Hunt, NHPA 33, 38 left
Anthony Huxley, NHPA jacket back, title page, 2-3 contents, 16-17, 18 top, 19, 20 bottom, 21 top, 22 top, 25, 31

bottom left, 63 left, 64
Peter Johnson, NHPA 51 top
F Naylor, NHPA 46 top, 47, 52, 53 top right
L Hugh Newman, NHPA 6, 10 top, 18 bottom, 69 top
New Zealand High Commission, 43
Ivan Polunin, NHPA jacket front, 22 bottom-23, 58-59, 62 right, 63 right top, 68 left
M Savonius, NHPA 9 bottom, 10 bottom, 45 top, 63 bottom, 67 bottom
Roy Shaw, NHPA 9 top
Tom Stack, NHPA 12, 27, 31 bottom right
James Tallon, NHPA 8 top